Put Your Heart Above Your Head

Releasing Kingdom Blessings

INCLUDING
THE SEVEN DAY CHALLENGE
TO DEVELOP A SERVANT'S HEART

Alemu Beeftu, Ph.D.
2010

Here's what other key leaders had to say about "Put Your Heart Above Your Head":

"Do you want to move up a notch in your personal life and in your service to God? If you do, remember what Jesus said: 'he who humbles himself will be exalted.' When God exalts you, He moves you up a notch! But how does this happen? Alemu Beeftu's wonderful book is a classic, simple instructional manual on personal humility. Read this book, follow Alemu's suggestions, and prepare to be exalted!"

C. PETER WAGNER, CHANCELLOR
WAGNER LEADERSHIP INSTITUTE

"Servant Leadership as a heart issue, in Alemu's vocabulary, means that to wash others' feet represents the core of following the footsteps of Jesus: that is, to die on the cross for others, no less and no more. Interestingly and truthfully, to serve others, to wash others' feet and to die for others, is a blessing, a fruitful path in our journey as leaders, a privileged path for learners."

BAMBANG BUDIJANTO, PH.D.
VICE PRESIDENT FOR ASIA REGION
COMPASSION INTERNATIONAL

"Highlighting the story of Jesus washing the disciples' feet, Alemu Beeftu details why we should follow the master's example and stoop down, thereby putting our hearts above our heads. He helps leaders identify the unique traits of the "Peters," "Judases," "Johns" and "Thomases" entrusted to our care, so we can serve and love them effectively and unconditionally. Only a secure leader sure of his or her calling will be humble enough to wash the feet of others. Drawing on personal experience and Biblical principles, Dr. Beeftu is a master teacher whose books always demand a practical response."

PAUL O'ROURKE, CEO
COMPASSION AUSTRALIA

"Washing the feet is generally seen as serving others, but Dr. Beeftu's radically different perception of the act as releasing is a welcome contribution to Christian understanding of leadership. The section on seven day prayer focus makes it a useful how-to-book for those committed to learning and teaching leadership that is Christ-like. I am delighted to recommend this book which brings the richness of Dr. Beeftu's years of experience to shape a highly readable contribution."

CB SAMUEL, LEADERSHIP MENTOR, INDIA

Put Your Heart Above Your Head

Releasing Kingdom Blessings

God Calls... Leaders Answer... The World Changes!

Published by Gospel of Glory, Prosper, TX USA.

The ministry of Gospel of Glory is to help build the Body of Christ by equipping leaders today in every strategic region of the world as well as bridging the gaps among Christian national leaders, the Body of Christ and emerging young leaders. Our mission is to develop, equip and empower leaders among the nations to serve God's purpose and impact their generations by providing biblically sound and culturally relevant books, leadership training workshops, seminars, and leadership accountability network teaching and mentoring.

It is our prayer that this book will help you to have daily relationship with Him in a pure heart so that you will be conformed into His image and reflect His glory in a greater measure.

For more information about resources from Gospel of Glory, please visit our website at www.gospelofglory.com or contact us at 972-347-5250.

Put Your Heart Above Your Head
© 2010 by Alemu Beeftu

ISBN 978-0-615-37949

First printing 2010
Printed in USA

Contents

Foreword

What are the traits of a great leader—a fluid orator with an imposing bearing and grand presence? In contrast to these worldly views, Jesus Christ's life and gospel are a testimony to how dissimilar God's perspective is on leadership.

Christ embodied God's perspective with a simple but profound act. On the eve of Christ's death, the bible finds Him kneeling at the feet of His disciples. This was not how Christ's disciples imagined their king and messiah—first on a donkey and then on His knees. Yet, so it is, that in Christ's humble form God committed all wisdom and knowledge on how to lead people; and, I believe such wisdom and knowledge flows over from ministry, to family, to school, to business, and to all facets of our existence.

Christ's *lowly* act of submissive leadership in John chapter 13 is preceded by our Lord's confirmation of the *heights* from whence He came: Jesus knew that the Father had put all things under his power, and that He had come from God and was returning to God; so he got up from the meal, took off his outer clothing, and wrapped a towel around his waist. After that, he poured water into a basin and began washing his disciple's feet.

Many cultures have stories of kings and leaders *acting* the part of paupers and slaves; invariably, however, in these stories the king is camouflaged or in disguise. Not our Christ! Here, we find him proclaiming his kingship as he removes his outer clothing and bends down to cleanse our dirty feet. There is no camouflage nor is there any deceit in Him.

It is a proclaimed king we find at our feet. Yet, no truer leader will any of us ever encounter. What a blessing it is to know this great truth. And what a blessing it is to find, in Dr. Alemu Beeftu's book, the perfect conduit to conform our lives to the hidden principles in Christ's simple act of leadership and submission. With insightful anecdotes and easily applicable lessons, Dr. Beeftu unbolts Christ's seemingly untenable, counter-intuitive and irrational act and reveals to his readers that Christ's path is in fact rational, intuitive, and deeply personal.

Fascinatingly, Dr. Beeftu also ably deconstructs the identities of the people whose feet Christ washes, lest we forget that Christ used an individual basin rather than a corporate tub. Christ knew God, He knew himself, *and* He knew each foot, where it had been and where it would be. So too should we intelligently and informatively approach our literal or figurative acts of submissive leadership.

Not only do I believe that Dr. Beeftu's work will greatly benefit ministers around the world, but business owners, educators, and parents will find surprising but effective means of crafting and sustaining effective leadership that will spawn not one but many leaders for and from this generation.

DR. BETTA MESGISTU, FOUNDER & PRESIDENT

BEZA INTERNATIONAL

Chapter One

PUTTING YOUR HEART
ABOVE YOUR HEAD

What does it mean to put your heart above your head? It was my privilege to hear this simple and straightforward teaching example from Bishop Joseph Garlington in early 2008.

Not long ago, a young woman—we'll call her Dina for our storytelling purposes—was in a very difficult childbirth. Despite the conveniences and technology of a modern hospital, the baby simply would not move through the birth canal.

The labor extended beyond hours into a day—then a day and a half. By then, the baby seemed to be stuck. As happens so often, the longer the labor extended, the more the mother and baby were at risk. Finally, in desperation, the young woman's father felt that they should call their hometown family physician, "Doc" Franks, for advice.

The attending physician agreed. If nothing else, the call would provide some comfort to the young woman and her parents, which would ease the tension for everyone else (including the young woman's husband) in the labor room.

A nurse dialed the number, then handed the phone to the attending doctor. "Dr. Franks? This is Dr. Emery at Central City General. I'm here with Dina Smithers; she used to be Dina Ward. You remember Dina? ... Good! Dina's having some issues delivering her baby. She's pretty much out of energy to push, the baby's stuck in the canal, and we're running out of time before I start the Caesarian. But the family wanted me to call you for any suggestions you might have ... I should what? Really? I think we can help her get into that position. Interesting idea, Dr. Franks. We'll try it! And no, I won't wait long at all if it doesn't work. Thanks!"

Dr. Emery sighed as he hung up the phone, and then gathered himself to direct the others in the room. "Nurse, help our mom-to-be sit up for just a moment. Dad, lower the bed so it's flat.... Good. Now I need both of you to be on either side of Dina. Help her kneel on the bed on all fours. Now, Dina, gently lower your head until it is lower than your heart. Let's hold it there for ten seconds or so. Take a break. Now another ten seconds. Keep your heart above your head, OK?"

After a few moments in the "heart above the head" position, the team helped Dina return to her normal delivery position. This time, when Dina pushed she got results. In short order, she delivered a tired but otherwise healthy baby boy.

Putting your heart above your head directs the blood to the brain, helping you to think more clearly and helping the brain to better respond to needs throughout the body. That's why when someone feels faint, the first step is to have them sit down and lower their head toward their knees. It restores the flow of blood to the head and revives them.

The Church today is much like Dina, trying with all her strength to give birth. But Dina needed an infusion of blood from her heart to her brain; then the brain could respond with clarity and vitality to the complex needs of the body during the birthing process.

Today, as the Church prepares to give birth to the next generation of the Kingdom, I believe we need to put our *"heart above our head."* We are not yet in a position to give birth. First we need genuine revival in this generation. We need to re-align ourselves so our relationship with Christ and with others is infused with fresh blood from the heart—Christ Himself.

This means we must examine, challenge, and set right the attitudes of our own hearts. And, we must recover a deep sense of calling that will allow us to lead as servants. We must recover the heart of Jesus—the heart of the ultimate Servant Leader—the One who showed us how to lead and serve by washing His followers' feet.

This simple book is about leading by washing the feet of others—not in the physical sense, but as a metaphor for serving. It examines the relationship between those who are washing feet (leaders) and those whose feet are washed (learners). It is honest and realistic about the challenge of serving those around you, and how the blessing of washing feet is not found in the ritual but in the relationships of those involved.

Therefore, *putting our heart above our head* is the way of practicing true and sincere humility, unconditional love, and forgiveness to help others to reach their destiny, as well as enjoying the freedom that comes through love and forgiveness. Let me illustrate this by an example of forgiveness from my wife Genet's life. This story is told in my book *Determination to Make a Difference,* a study of the Book of Ruth:

Most students in Ethiopia hadn't attended school for almost three years due to the Communist takeover of the country. It was the end of 1978, in the city of Addis Ababa. We were very excited and hopeful that we could return to our schools. However, the students began to protest against the new Communist government. Students would stone to death whoever didn't participate in the opposition. Yet the government threatened to kill those who protested. Since my fellow students were always around me, I joined the student protesters.

The very day I joined, soldiers came and chased us with fire truck hoses and tear gas. Everyone ran as fast and as far as possible. I fell down and the fleeing students ran over me. I finally was able to get up, and I ran to a small two-room house.

A woman at the door said, "Please don't come into my house, as I have no place to hide you. And I don't want you killed in my house." I promised that I'd go outside if someone came to kill me. She didn't listen, and kept crying for me not to come inside. At the same time, four more girls ran up to her house, so then there were five of us. We all ran into her house, but there was no place to hide.

Finally, I slid under a very low bed. A soldier then rushed into the house and grabbed three of the girls. The fourth girl picked up the lady's baby and pretended to nurse the baby. The soldier thought she was the baby's mother and didn't question her. The soldier then looked under the bed and said to me, "You better come out."

The woman replied, "You are taking three girls, so let this one go home to tell the parents to look for their missing daughters."

He said, "If I take her I won't harm her, but if someone else comes after me and takes her, she will be tortured." The woman told him, "It's OK. She will be fine. Just don't take her." He left me under the bed.

After a short while another soldier stormed into the house and said to me, "I am going to count to three, and if you don't come out I will shoot."

He began to count and the woman started screaming, "I don't want to see blood! Oh God, please don't let this happen in my house!"

I then told him I would come out. They lifted the bed and I stood up. He began to slap and kick me. He also started hitting my joints with a billy club to keep me from running off. He kicked me hard in my right side and I passed out.

The next thing I remembered was being thrown into a truck with other students. The truck and driver had been taken over by the Communists and were being used to haul students to a nearby prison. I woke up while in the truck. I could see we were driving through my neighborhood and saw my house. Seeing my home, I prayed, "God, if you're there, I pray that you'll be with my family— especially my sister. If they hear that I'm killed tonight, please comfort them."

I then thought that God must not care. If He did, He wouldn't have let this happen. There were 92 of us students in the truck being hauled to the prison, and many were badly injured from beatings and torture. Some were bleeding.

When we reached the prison, they told us to sit outside on the ground. It was wet and muddy from raining all day. We were told they would be taking our pictures, and we would have to sign a document that stated, "Because I protested against the government, I deserve to be punished by red terror. I show my agreement to be punished by signing this document."

Red terror meant being shot and killed. At this point the fear of being tortured and killed had left, as there was no hope of being released. Anger and hate had settled in my heart. As we waited for the process to unfold, they took our individual pictures and forced us to sign the document. We began to mentally prepare to be brave and face death. They kept us outside the prison until evening.

Around 8:00 p.m., the captain ordered us to come individually into his office to call our parents to come, sign for us, and take us home! When he said this, we all thought it was simply a way for him to kill us individually. We all told him to kill us in the group—not individually. He kept telling us to come to his office, so we could call our parents. I stood up and told him that if he planned to kill us, I wanted to be first. But if it were true that we could call our parents, then I would be first to make a phone call.

As I walked toward his office, everyone shouted that I was crazy! While walking, I closed my eyes and said, "OK, shoot and get it over with." He appeared sad upon hearing this, and told me to sit down and call my parents. He said he wouldn't harm me. It was hard for me to believe his kind words, as I had heard he was very cruel.

I called my parents. Our maid said they had been waiting to hear from the officials. By the time I was released from the prison, it was 10:00 p.m. Usually the government would kill prisoners at midnight. The captain released us before that hour, so when the killing squad came through we were gone.

It was later reported that about 6,000 students were taken from prisons throughout the city that night and were shot to death. When the captain released us, he told us to stay in hiding for a year, so we wouldn't be recognized. Although we were told this, the next day I joined friends to attend funerals for several of our classmates.

The captain who released us from prison was killed the next day for freeing us from the prison and for destroying our documents.

This was an extremely difficult time for me, as I wanted to finish my education and fulfill my goals. But the schools were now closed, and I was supposed to be in hiding.

I went into hiding at my cousin's home in a missionary compound where no one knew me. I had to keep distant from my family. I was very angry with God and couldn't understand why this was happening. I didn't think God loved us, since He allowed students to be killed.

"Life" was filled with mental torture. I came to a point where I rejected God because He wasn't stopping the horrible atrocities. My heart filled with anger and hatred. I hated every soldier on earth. I hated the Communists. I was consumed with rage and revenge. Day and night all I thought of was how to get revenge against the soldiers, the government, and the Communists.

Because of my anger and bitterness, I lost my appetite and nights were sleepless. Every time I heard the government had killed someone, the anger and hatred grew deeper. At this time my uncle was killed along with 60 ministers of the king of Ethiopia. Later my uncle's son and daughter, my cousins, were killed. Following this, the government arrested my father, as they feared he would seek revenge for the death of his brother, my uncle.

For about four years tragic events took place within most families in our city. From 1976 to early

1979 were very difficult years for everyone. These were the years the government declared "red terror" on anyone they disliked, especially if the family was wealthy.

During the late 1970s the schools opened again, so I returned home and finished school. I also took evening classes at the university. In the meantime, my younger sister went to Germany to get medical help for a physical problem. After living in Germany for three years, she went to the United States. Once there, she applied for scholarships at colleges for our youngest sister and me. The Lord opened a door for us to attend Fresno Pacific College in Fresno, California. We arrived there in 1982.

That summer, the Lord began dealing with my anger and bitterness. Because of the hurt and bitterness, I lost my appetite and couldn't sleep. One morning while I was having devotions, I prayed to the Lord, "Please help me. I need to eat or I'll get sick and die."

While praying, I felt as though the brutal soldier who had attacked me had entered the room. I was frightened, so I opened my eyes to see if he was there. I then heard an audible voice say,

"Healing is in your hands. Forgive, and you will want to eat again."

I wondered who was talking to me. It didn't make sense. "There's no way I would forgive a man who made my life miserable! I will not forgive him." While thinking these things, I felt the deep hurt and started to weep. Then I prayed, "Lord, you can't expect me to forgive as simply as this. They don't deserve to be forgiven. Did you forget what they did?"

I then started telling the Lord everything the Communists had done to my family, my country, and me. I stood up and said, "I can't do it, Lord. I would rather starve than forgive the Communists."

But the Holy Spirit kept challenging me. Every day I felt the urge to forgive, but I wouldn't. One day as I was having devotions, I remembered the verse that says, "For if you forgive men their trespasses, your heavenly Father will also forgive you. But if you do not forgive men their trespasses, neither will your Father forgive your trespasses" (Matthew 6:14-15). When I read this verse, I thought, "It's not fair! Not fair at all! Why should I forgive them when they don't deserve it? They only deserve revenge and judgment—not forgiveness!"

At this point another verse came to mind: "It is mine to avenge; I will repay..." (Deuteronomy 32:35). Then I said, "Lord, how can I do this? How can I forgive them? Lord, I want to obey You, but I don't know how. I want to forgive, but I can't. I just can't do it!"

Right after saying this, I felt the hand of the Lord lift from my heart all the hurt, anger, and bitterness that had consumed my life. I began weeping and finally felt free. The stronghold of bitterness was broken. My spirit was free and a weight was lifted from me. I felt light and relaxed, as all the heavy tightness was gone. I even began praying for the Communist government and for the soldiers who were so brutal. My heart was changed.

What a surprise!

After praying, I was hungry and ate as never before. That night I slept through the night for the first time in four years. The Lord had healed me and began to restore me. I felt the Lord's healing hand upon me each day, guiding and leading me forward. I sensed I was not to look back and pick up the old hurts and wounds, but to move forward with Him in victory.

Once the decision was made to forgive, the process of forgiveness began. Forgiveness is a process that requires a daily decision not to look back and dwell on past experiences. Because a person has spent considerable time in self-pity when in an unforgiving state, a decision must be made to not look back at the past. Otherwise it's easy to fall back into bitterness and justify that previous, familiar state of mind.

After a period of time, the Lord began challenging me to share my experience of forgiving my enemies. At first I found this uncomfortable, as I would have to verbally acknowledge before others that I had forgiven the soldiers and other Communists. Public confession of having forgiven brutality and murder was difficult.

Gradually the Lord made my healing complete and victorious. Glory, honor and praise to Him! Amen! I have since promised the Lord that, with His help, I will not hold grudges or get bitter toward those who may wrong me. This is a difficult promise to keep, but with His grace I have held to this promise. Tests come almost daily, but nothing is impossible with Him and in Him.

Praise His Holy Name!

When the flesh says "revenge," the Spirit says "forgiveness." Genet is a living testimony of the power of forgiveness. From her example, I have learned that God does not ask that we deny the reality of past hurts—but He does require us to move past them if we are to fulfill His calling on our lives. It was the same for Naomi. It is the same for you and me regarding footwashing. We must understand that we are also going against what is natural to do what is spiritual.

The chapters that follow offer you a pattern that may help you make footwashing (in its relational sense) an everyday way of life that can continually bring Kingdom blessings to you and those around you. Yet the goal is not the blessing, but the opportunity to bring God glory through our lives of service to Him. May God bless you as you pursue this challenge to follow our Lord's example and make footwashing a source of both service and blessing!

"Surely God is good to Israel,
to those who are pure in heart."
Psalm 73:1

Chapter Two

JESUS' LAST LESSON

t was just before the Passover Feast. Jesus knew that the time had come for him to leave this world and go to the Father. Having loved his own who were in the world, he now showed them the full extent of his love. The evening meal was being served, and the devil had already prompted Judas Iscariot, son of Simon, to betray Jesus. Jesus knew that the Father had put all things under his power, and that he had come from God and was returning to God; so he got up from the meal, took off his outer clothing, and wrapped a towel around his waist. After that, he poured water into a basin and began to wash his disciples' feet, drying them with the towel that was wrapped around him. (John 13:1-5)

The Lord Jesus went into the Jordan River to be baptized by John to start his ministry. When He came out of the water and prayed, the heavens were opened and He was anointed for ministry — the Holy Spirit came upon Him and the Father spoke from heaven. Then by the power of the Holy Spirit and the word of God, He overcame the temptation of the evil one in the desert.

After that Jesus went to the mountain and prayed all night long before he chose the twelve.

Jesus went up into the hills and called to him those he wanted, and they came to him. He appointed twelve— designating them apostles—that they might be with him and that he might send them out to preach and to have authority to drive out demons. (Mark 3:13-15)

From day one of His public ministry, the Lord Jesus trained the twelve disciples for leadership. He gave them power and authority to drive out demons and cure diseases as signs of their apostolic calling. Their mission was to advance the Kingdom.

After more than three years of personal training, discipling, and equipping, their graduation day came. None of them seemed ready for it. Regardless, the Lord Jesus was ready to go to the cross. In hours, He would pay the price of the sins of the world. Mere weeks later, He would go back to the Father. He had His last Passover supper on earth with them. It marked the final practical training class (or we might call it a graduation ceremony) that summarized the three years of practical training they had received.

A Final Challenge

That night, Jesus took precious time to do something curious and startling. Out of His great love for the disciples—all twelve of them—and knowing that the full power of the Father was at His disposal, Jesus washed their feet.

Throughout His ministry, Jesus had challenged His disciples' beliefs and attitudes as He demonstrated a revolutionary model for life and ministry. Now, washing His followers' feet, Jesus again turned upside down His society's (and His disciples') ideas of leadership, social and religious status, relationship, and servanthood. Jesus was their rabbi, their leader, their Lord. Footwashing violated their understanding of these roles. It was a lowly servant's job; proper society despised the task.

Yes, the disciples were shocked that Jesus would lower Himself in such a way (i.e. putting His heart above His head). But they didn't know at the time the depth of Jesus' humility. Only Jesus knew the unconditional love, acceptance, and forgiveness He was demonstrating.

- Jesus bowed to wash His disciples' feet with full knowledge that they would abandon

19

Him—betray Him, deny Him, and run away in fear—that very night.

• Jesus performed this humble act of service regardless of His disciples' individual character flaws and failures. He served them equally, whether they loved Him, doubted Him, denied Him, or were ready to crucify Him.

• Jesus knew the disciples didn't yet share His agenda of leading through serving. They still expected Him to become a powerful political leader. They awaited that revelation so they could begin to share in His power. They had no idea that Jesus would make footwashing a means of developing effective leadership.

Knowing all this, Jesus knelt at their feet.

This unusual final encounter with Jesus was significant in many ways. We will examine this thoroughly in Chapter 3, but let's take a brief look at why Jesus chose footwashing as His final lesson to His disciples.

First, Jesus' footwashing expressed the cleansing and purification needed for the disciples to be set apart and consecrated for ministry.

20

Second, it was a demonstration of Jesus' deep love and care for them, His unconditional acceptance of them as they were, and His recognition of who they would become as leaders in the Church.

Third, it prepared the disciples to transition into leadership as apostles. Jesus showed them that power and authority can be manifested through servanthood; He provided an ultimate model of servant leadership for the disciples to follow; and He demonstrated that leadership is fundamentally and essentially relational.

Finally, Jesus' act was a declaration of their final destiny, a qualifying act to remind the disciples to follow His footsteps in humility, authority, and service.

A TWO-WAY STREET

Servant leadership is a two-way street. In one direction, leaders shape their followers. In the other direction—and one just as formative—followers develop their leaders.

It's important that we understand and value this two-way dynamic and how it affects the

21

decisions leaders must make to effectively wash the feet of those God has entrusted to their care.

The Father didn't give Jesus the "best and brightest" of first century Palestine as His first disciples. These were flawed men. Peter had a temper. James and John were mama's boys, constantly jockeying for position. Thomas was a cynic. Judas Iscariot was a petty thief and classic manipulator. Simon the Zealot was a political extremist. The others had their issues, too.

Yet each of these flawed individuals contributed to the fulfillment of Jesus' mission. The question for us is, "How will the flawed individuals I serve help me fulfill the calling God has for me?" Consider these possibilities:

- People like John will support and stand by you in your time of need and difficulties;

- People like Peter will teach you daily forgiveness and unconditional love;

- People like Thomas will help you "walk straight" with integrity of character;

- People like Judas will help you die to self to fulfill your destiny;

- Others help you learn to trust the Lord no matter what the circumstances.

These types of people are given to a leader for the character-building process servant leadership requires. Washing the feet of such people in your life is an indication of your willingness to learn from them.

This does not lessen their responsibility to learn from you. A biblical depiction of submitting to teaching is "sitting at one's feet." Sitting at someone's feet, with an attitude of respect, expresses a desire to humbly receive instruction for a life journey. Mary chose to sit at the feet of Jesus to receive divine revelation and instruction. Jesus said that what she received would never be taken from her. Clearly, sitting at someone's feet is a choice that leads to lasting blessing, especially as the learning leads to action.

Whether you are a leader or a learner (and sometimes you're both), washing feet is an action that should lead to blessings. Foot washing is a process that releases eternal blessing that no one will take away. *You know these things, and God will bless you, if you do them.* (John 13:17, CEV)

23

Washing feet is about one's heart condition and attitude transformation. Being on our hands and knees is a reflection of our heart condition. Washing feet is not about the quality of character of individuals we serve, but is rather a reflection of *our* character and purity of heart. It is a measurement of our worship, spiritual authority, and eternal love for God and others.

FURTHER WORD ABOUT FEET

Feet, themselves, are humble servants. They carry our full weight. They take us where we need to go. They help us do what needs to be done. They are a measure of reality, connecting our body to the earth. Feet don't make decisions; they follow orders. And in the process they endure heat, dust, dirt, moisture, cold, and a lot of aches and pains. Shouldn't we treat them with gratitude and honor, the way Jesus treated the feet of the disciples? I've heard people describe feet as ugly and "yucky." But God has a different view of feet. To Him, our feet can be absolutely beautiful. Let's explore how God evaluates the beauty of our feet.

24

Chapter Three

BEAUTIFUL FEET

H *ow beautiful on the mountains are the feet of those who bring good news, who proclaim peace, who bring good tidings, who proclaim salvation, who say to Zion, "Your God reigns!"* (Isaiah 52:7)

BEAUTIFUL FEET ON THE MOUNTAINS

The Hebrew word for beauty is *na'ah*. It means "to be comely, to be beautiful, to be befitting."[1] So, restating the verse above, "How beautiful, how comely, suitable and fitting, are of the feet of good news messengers."

What should the feet of a good news messenger look like? In broad brushstrokes, the beauty of their feet is about holiness of life, purity of heart (being clean), and character qualities (such as splendor, magnificence, and loveliness). In this context, "feet" represent the total person: spirit, soul, and body. When someone has beautiful feet like these, they are suitable for a leadership role. So how can we encourage the development of beautiful feet from God's perspective?

The process of cleansing is of primary importance. Cleansing removes what shouldn't be there, thus enhancing purity. The Bible talks about both enhancing purity and washing. In the Old Testament the Lord asked leaders to remove their shoes. In the New Testament Jesus literally washed the feet of the twelve apostles.

Throughout the Word of God, feet are used as symbols and metaphors. Scripture tells us that, in creation, the Lord placed everything under our feet. (Psalm 8:6; Hebrews 2:8). That signifies power and authority for dominion. He promised Joshua that every place the soles of their feet trod, He would give to them as inheritance. This, again, is a picture of authority and dominion.

The Lord promised to put our enemies under the soles of our feet (Malachi 4:3). In a literal sense, when Joshua conquered the five kings, he asked the leaders to place their feet on the kings' necks and killed them as a sign of final victory (Joshua 10:23-24). King Solomon figuratively referred to King David's victories by saying that the Lord put David's enemies under his feet (1 Kings 5:3).

Furthermore, God the Father promised the Lord Jesus Christ to put his enemies under His feet: *The Lord said to my Lord: "Sit at my right hand until I put your enemies under your feet"* (Matthew 22:44). In talking about the victory of the Lord Jesus, Paul put it this way: *And God placed all things under his feet and appointed him to be head over everything for the church* ... (Ephesians 1:22). The Lord even promised to crush Satan under the feet of believers as a sign of victory (Romans 16:20).

It's also important to understand the significance of oil and mountains in reference to beautiful feet. The Bible tells us about bathing feet in oil (Deuteronomy 33:24). Jesus' feet were bathed in precious oil in preparation for His sacrificial ministry. Oil is about anointing, which signifies and imparts both consecration and authority. Anointing also indicates being set apart for an assignment with responsibility and authority. That is what makes the feet of those who bring good news on the mountain beautiful.

The mountain of God is where the cloud of His glorious presence dwells. It can be any mountain; the key is that God's presence is there. For example, Moses was likely on Mt. Sinai for forty days with the

Lord. When he came down from that mountain, Moses' face was shining with the glory of the Lord (Exodus 34). The prophets talked about the house of God being the mountain for nations to come and see. The mountain's location is not as crucial as it being the place of the Lord's presence: *In the last days the mountain of the Lord's temple will be established as chief among the mountains; it will be raised above the hills, and all nations will stream to it* (Isaiah 2:2).

Therefore, the beauty of feet on the mountain of God results from coming from His presence to declare His will and eternal purpose.

TAKE OFF YOUR SHOES, PART ONE

In the past few years, airline passengers have been asked to remove their shoes as part of the routine security check before boarding. It can be a frustrating process that seems to take too much time, yet it has a vital purpose: to check where a passenger's feet have been.

X-rays can screen for items of concern that might be detected inside shoes. Modern technology also allows security officers to blow a puff of air on the shoes and immediately screen for chemicals. This reveals, to some extent, where the shoes have traveled in the past and can warn of potential danger for fellow passengers.

The Holy Spirit does a similar check to reveal where a leader's feet have walked. For example, God revealed time and again that the behavior of King Saul, from cheating on sacrifices to seeking counsel from the witch at Endor, was endangering the people of Israel. When David sinned with Bathsheba, the Spirit of God spoke to the prophet Nathan to reveal the impact of David's sin on the people around him and, ultimately, the nation he led.

It is crucial that leaders avoid going to places— physical, emotional, or spiritual—that threaten the wellbeing of those they lead. You simply can't cleanse the harmful traces of where you've been without divine intervention.

This said, there are other reasons that might make you take off your shoes for the joy of what's ahead.

TAKE OFF YOUR SHOES, PART TWO

Our relationship with God is by grace, because of His wonderful mercy. The mercy of God revises the judgment we deserve. Grace provides undeserved provision to qualify us to have access to His presence. Grace places us in everlasting relationship with God, the Creator and the Redeemer. God's total package of revised judgment, released and undeserved forgiveness, and His love signifies His favor is being released.

God's favor is what qualifies us to lead others and to fulfill His purpose on earth as an ambassador of His Kingdom. This is the core of biblical leadership. There is also a cost to biblical leadership we must consider.

The cost of representing God on earth begins with personal holiness. Holiness is to be set apart for God. The fundamental issue in being set apart as an ambassador of God's Kingdom is *letting go of things that hold us back.*

Abraham was the first leader in the Bible who was told to let go of his country, his people, and his father's household. God's mission was for Abraham to be a father and leader of nations. In obedience to God's calling, Abraham let go of everything and became a friend of God, a father of many nations, and a blessing to all humanity.

The second such leader was Moses. Moses knew his call and embraced it with his whole heart. He waited for the right timing to lead God's people to freedom. Moses was willing to pay the full price for his leadership call. The first thing Moses let go for the sake of his leadership was the pleasure of Egypt (Hebrews 11:24-27). This pleasure includes the privilege he had as a grandson of Pharaoh, the king of Egypt. With this he also rejected the honor that came with social status: his title, his name, his Egyptian power and authority. For Moses, all these were temporary. They didn't relate to his destiny. Moses not only refused the pleasure of Egypt, but also "...chose to be mistreated along with the people of God rather than to enjoy the pleasures of sin for a short time" (Hebrews 11:25).

After Moses waited 80 years for the Lord, the Lord revealed Himself to him. However, before God would commission Moses, He asked the prophet to take off his shoes: ... *God called to him from within the bush, "Moses! Moses!" And Moses said, "Here I am." "Do not come any closer," God said. "Take off your sandals, for the place where you are standing is holy ground"* (Exodus 3:4-5).

Moses' shoes represented 80 years of life experience, including:

- A sense of failure, because after he killed an Egyptian to help his people their situation became worse;

- Fear, as he ran from Pharaoh simply to stay alive instead of improving his people's lot in Egypt;

- Rejection, as the Hebrews in Egypt refused to recognize him as a person, much less a leader. As a result, Moses became a shepherd of his father-in-law's sheep in the wilderness, ignorant of his future and the future of his people.

This is why the first thing the Lord asked Moses, before commissioning him as a leader of his people, was to take off his shoes: *Moses had to let go the past for the sake of his future.* Taking off his shoes would signify exactly that for Moses. Once those shoes were off, Moses was ready to take good news of deliverance to the nation of Israel, who had been under a heavy yoke of oppression for more than 400 years. By asking Moses to take off his shoes, the Lord was saying to Moses, "Let go of any part of your past that might hinder your effectiveness."

Taking off one's shoes also speaks about holy reverence (worship, awe, respect, fear) for God. This was certainly the case with Moses, who took off his shoes and covered his face in holy reverence to the manifested presence of God—making the desert of Horeb holy ground.

Now as then, taking off one's old shoes also allows the right kind of shoes to take their place with authority as well as readiness: *And having shod your feet in preparation [to face the enemy with the firm-footed stability, the promptness, and the readiness produced by the good news] of the Gospel of peace* (Ephesians 6:15, AMP).

The angel of the Lord asked Joshua a very similar thing. After Moses' death, Joshua took leadership and prepared the people to enter and possess the land of their inheritance. After they crossed the river Jordan, before they destroyed city of Jericho, the commander of the army of the Lord stood before Joshua. Joshua asked the angel, "Are you for us or for our enemies?" (Joshua 5:13). His answer was "neither." When Joshua asked him what message he had for them, the *commander of the Lord's army replied, "Take off your sandals, for the place where you are standing is holy." And Joshua did so* (Joshua

33

5:15). In this case again, Joshua's removal of his shoes was about reverence, submission, and letting go of 40 years of wilderness experience. To face Jericho (and all the enemies they fought after Jericho) and to possess the land, Joshua had to remove his old shoes. That way, he could walk in authority for victory.

In this sense, it is crucial that a leader take off things that might hinder running God's race and accomplishing God's purpose. For example, David took off Saul's armor before he went and killed Goliath, the enemy of the people of God.

Taking off old shoes is also a sign of coming freedom. After the Lord raised Lazarus from death, He told those who were responsible to take off Lazarus' grave clothes, which reflected the place that, a few moments before, held Lazarus captive: *The dead man came out, his hands and feet wrapped with strips of linen, and a cloth around his face. Jesus said to them, "Take off the grave clothes and let him go"* (John 11:44). Jesus commanded that they take off what was a sign of death. Then as now, a culture of unbelief could bury what was intended for the glory of God.

Furthermore, taking off shoes shows the beautiful feet that will provide the footprints a generation can see clearly and follow. The Word of God talks about the feet of a leader far more than the face of a leader. A leader's feet tell the story of a walk through life or life experiences. The authority of a leader comes far more from having beautiful feet than a beautiful face.

In the case of the disciples, Jesus washed their feet to give them feet beautiful enough to qualify them for the New Testament leadership. In their case, as in the case of anyone who would be the Lord's messenger, the question is, "How beautiful, suitable, and fitting are your feet?"

"*And David shepherded them with integrity of heart; with skillful hands he led them.*"

Psalm 78:72

Chapter Four

WHY FOOTWASHING?

*Jesus answered, "Unless I wash you, you
have no part in me."* (John 13:8)

As we discussed earlier, Jesus' decision to wash
the disciples' feet was deeply significant in
what it manifested and demonstrated as a
final lesson in servanthood and leadership. We
would do well to consider Jesus' example carefully
and thoughtfully in the context of our ministry to
others.

1. **Washing feet expressed Jesus' love.** *Having loved
his own who were in the world, he now showed them
the full extent of his love.* (John 13:1) Though He
was their Lord, Jesus washed the disciples' feet,
showing them the limitlessness of His love. This
proved to the disciples that Jesus' love is not
bound by place or condition. He didn't reserve
His love until they were filled with the Holy
Spirit, endowed as apostles, and winning souls
to His kingdom. He loved them when they were

overcome by doubts and fear, angry with each other, and complaining about their circumstances. In this episode of His ministry, Jesus Christ showed practically that God remains unshaken in His love for us. Ministry is about unconditional love in all its many forms and expressions.

The power of God's love stems from its intrinsic nature, here described in 1 Corinthians 13, 4-7:

> Love is patient, love is kind. It does not envy, it does not boast, it is not proud. It is not rude, it is not self-seeking, it is not easily angered, it keeps no record of wrongs. Love does not delight in evil but rejoices with the truth. It always protects, always trusts, always hopes, always perseveres.

God does not use the person who shows conditional, transient love. Instead, He uses the person who submits himself to lasting love, the way Jesus Christ did. "... and over all these virtues put on love, which binds them all together in perfect unity" (Colossians 3:14).

As you minister, you many have the occasion to ask some (or all) of the following questions. Notice how love answers them all:

- *Question: What do I do if others undermine my ministry as I kneel down to wash their feet in service?* Answer: Carry on with your ministry in love to the last.

- *Question: What do I do when those I lovingly serve gossip about me?* Answer: Love and serve them whether you are comfortable with them or not.

- *Question: What do I do when they misunderstand my motives, wrongly considering that what I do is to gain advantages?* Answer: Faithfully carry on to the last with your ministry in love, proving to them you really love them and are justified only by God.

- *Question: What do I do when I see they do not notice or care about what is necessary for me: food, shelter, and other needs?* Answer: Remember the One who called you knows your needs. He is your hope. Hold onto His love to the last.

- *Question: What do I do when I am fed up and angry at their negligence?* Answer: Intercede for them with mercy and love.

2. **Washing feet confirmed His authority.** *Jesus knew that the Father had put all things under his power, and that he had come from God and was returning to God.* (John 13:3) The depth of the servant's spiritual authority is measured by the servant's humility and attitude regarding ministry. Once a leader discerns the genuine spiritual authority of the Most High, the leader must kneel in respect and holy fear. Leaders must also demonstrate humility toward others as part of their response to God.

   Moses lived a humble life because he understood the greatness of spiritual authority. Stephen died interceding for those who stoned him to death because he knew the depth of spiritual authority. Having understood this secret, Paul forcefully subdued his flesh to the will of God. Jesus Christ bowed to wash His disciples' feet because He knew the essence of spiritual authority.

Do we understand this mystery? If we do, to what extent do we understand? Let us measure the depth of our understanding by our ability to leave our leadership "throne," kneeling down before God and those we serve with a genuine feeling of joy.

3. **Washing feet revealed His glory.** *Jesus knew that the Father had put all things under his power, and that he had come from God and was returning to God* ... (John 13:3) Jesus Christ became flesh, having left His great glory with the Father in heaven (Philippians 2:5-11). Because Jesus knew the end of His ministry on earth was near and He was on the threshold of resuming His glory in heaven, He washed His disciples' feet after supper. Washing the disciples' feet did not diminish His glory in any way because His glory came from heaven and His Father. So too, when we discern our honor in the eyes of the Lord, we can leave our seats, tie our waist with the belt of truth, and serve. Temporal, human-bestowed honor cannot satisfy the person who has a deep understanding of the heavenly, eternal glory.

4. **Washing feet gave a practical demonstration of His teachings.** As mentioned before, when Jesus

41

washed the feet of His disciples He once again—hopefully once and for all—turned upside down their ideas of leadership, social and religious status, relationship, and servanthood. This startling act of service was the culmination of His training and mentoring process. If the disciples had somehow missed the point of the parables, the Sermon on the Mount, Jesus' compassionate, restorative touch, His utter submission to the Father, and His conversations with the sin-sick and broken—He would show them one, final time.

> *Do you understand what I have done for you? ... Now that I, your Lord and Teacher, have washed your feet, you also should wash one another's feet. I have set you an example that you should do as I have done for you. I tell you the truth, no servant is greater than his master, nor is a messenger greater than the one who sent him. Now that you know these things, you will be blessed if you do them.*(John 13:12-17)

The level of our ministry is measured not only by serving with our gifts, but also by living the truth of God. God wants and uses such servants.

5. **Washing feet demonstrated the godly value of serving**. Jesus, serving in such a humble way, demonstrated the difference between God's thoughts and our thoughts. When Jesus Christ came as the Messiah, the Jews expected Him to deliver them from oppression and exploitation from the Romans and endow them with political liberty. But God's plan was to provide them with internal freedom—an emancipation of the heart—prior to their external liberation. When Jesus entered Jerusalem seated on a donkey, the Jews cried, "Hosanna!" It seemed to be a political outcry: "Set us free right away!" But Jesus went to Jerusalem to be a sacrifice, a Passover Lamb, for their sin and the sin of all mankind. Even His disciples did not expect His death. They, too, were looking to the coronation of a king.

Jesus Christ provided a clear, practical demonstration of genuine service. He established the pattern of New Testament ministry. He exemplified ministry that pleases God and became the servant who attracts God's attention. The Jews expected a ministry where the Messiah would set out on a journey of conquests, carrying the banner of freedom lifted high, symbolizing victory over all foes and being a king ruling over the liberated kingdom of Israel. In contrast, Jesus Christ lifted a towel of ministry that He used to dry the feet of His own disciples.

Ministry does not begin with liberating others, but with first being liberated. Our own liberation in Christ allows us to serve and liberate others. Even if a man is not truly free inside, it would be possible for him to lift high a visible, colorful banner and gain a following. But it would be difficult for him to take a towel and kneel down in front of others. He who carries a banner rushes ahead of others. But he who takes a towel kneels before others. The cloth of New Testament ministry forms not a banner, but a towel. Whatever the circumstances of our mission, our call is to touch, clean, beautify, console, inspire with hope, and build.

The Jews knew that the high priest used oil to anoint the king for them. But Jesus Christ did not wait for this anointing. Instead, He knelt down, taking water to wash others' feet. God the Father anointed Him to serve others: *For even the Son of*

Man did not come to be served, but to serve, and to give his life as a ransom for many (Mark 10:45). Jesus exemplified the New Testament call and service. His anointing required Him to make others clean.

6. **Washing feet illustrated the kind of person God wants to use.** In the act of washing others' feet, Jesus Christ demonstrated not merely the essence of genuine ministry, but also how to be the type of person God wants to use. He used this humble act to teach us that ministry reflects not only those who are served; ministry primarily reflects the nature of the servant.

In other words, we give service not because we are always comfortable or pleased with those we serve and are always desirous of serving them, but because God has changed our hearts and filled us with love and humility. This is the lesson Jesus gives us.

Consider the variety of personalities among the men whose feet Jesus washed—and, likewise, the variety of people we serve. We will wash their feet for these reasons:

a. To demonstrate the character of Jesus in us;

b. To develop the character of Jesus in us;

c. To bless those we serve;

d. To be an example of godly servant-leadership;

e. To confront those we serve with love.

In the coming chapters, we will examine how these elements interact with each other in the task of washing the feet of the variety of people God has charged us to lead and serve.

Chapter Five

WASHING JOHN'S FEET

N ear the cross of Jesus stood his mother, his
mother's sister, Mary the wife of Clopas, and
Mary Magdalene. When Jesus saw his mother
there, and the disciple whom he loved standing nearby, he
said to his mother, "Dear woman, here is your son," and
to the disciple, "Here is your mother." From that time on,
this disciple took her into his home. (John 19:25-27)

WHO WAS JOHN FOR JESUS?

The Lord Jesus called John from the
marketplace to be His disciple. John was fishing at
the Sea of Galilee with his father, Zebedee, and his
brother, James, when Jesus called both of the
brothers to follow Him (Matthew 4:18-22). The
house of Zebedee must have had a prosperous
fishing business because Mark's gospel (1:19-20)
notes that the brothers left the hired men behind in
the boats with their father. Indeed, historians like
William Barclay note that the house of Zebedee

supplied fish for some clientele of note in Jerusalem — including the house of Herod.[2]

John was not a naïve, trusting, and mindless soul. He came from a family of shrewd businessmen who were used to, within boundaries, profiting from every relationship. This "What's in it for me?" aspect of the Beloved Disciple (as John was known) is clearly noted in several gospel accounts, including the argument over who would be seated next to Jesus when His Kingdom was consummated (Mark 10:35-45). Yet as he followed Jesus, John cast away selfish expectations in exchange for the determination to be faithful.

John, Peter, and James became the closest circle of Jesus' followers. They were with Jesus when He healed Jairus' daughter. They joined Him on the Mount of Transfiguration (Mark 9:2-13), even hearing the voice of God the Father from a cloud. Yet perhaps more telling is the fact that John, alone among the twelve disciples, was present at the foot of Jesus' cross during His crucifixion.

There at the cross, the remarkable story of John gains a powerful dynamic. Noting both his mother

Mary and his faithful disciple John among those with Him as He died, Jesus said to Mary, "Here is your son." To John, Jesus said, "Here is your mother." Think of it: *at that moment, Jesus trusted John so much that He could commit His own mother to his friend.*

John exemplified a life of commitment and covenant friendship. He was characterized by love, faithfulness, dependability, and trustworthiness. Jesus loved John as an exceptionally faithful friend and follower (John 13:23).

Well after His ascension, Jesus revealed Himself to John on the Isle of Patmos, as recorded in the Book of Revelation. John was faithful during persecution, isolation, and harsh circumstances. Even then, John's focus was still on the Lord Jesus Christ's love: *...To him who loves us and has freed us from our sins by his blood* ... (Revelation 1:5). In fact, John was in the Spirit, focusing on the price the Lord paid because of His love: *On the Lord's Day I was in the Spirit...* (Revelation 1:10).

John was a loving, kind, determined, faithful, and reliable apostle. If it was necessary to wash someone's feet, John's might be the easiest to wash. However, it would be a tragically limited view of

49

ministry to choose to serve only people like John (those with whom we feel comfortable), and leaving others out. The New Testament call isn't about our comfort level.

WHO IS JOHN FOR YOU?

Who is John for you? John represents a covenant person who will be there for you no matter what. Look for these characteristics in the people around you:

- A faithful, but not blind, follower or friend;
- Someone who has "marketplace skills;"
- Someone who has chosen to develop a deep relationship with you;
- Someone with whom you feel comfortable;
- Someone you think, either today or in the future, could take your place in one or more important ways.

WASHING JOHN'S FEET

Jesus washed John's feet to affirm a covenant relationship, and to purify and cleanse John for greater responsibility. When the Lord gives us a faithful person, it is very important that we nurture

50

the relationship. God has prepared a person like John for every leader. However, if it took Jesus three years to produce a faithful friend like John who could be trusted even at one's death, it might take us longer.

Therefore, our first challenge is *the willingness to put in the time it will take to build a covenant relationship.* It will certainly require some work; even for the Lord it took work and patience to develop John from the Sea of Galilee to the island of Patmos. It may be easy to see John's potential, but the finished product may take years.

The second challenge is that of *understanding both the price and process of covenant relationship.* An example of this process of covenant relationship is what we read in Ruth 1:16-18:

> *But Ruth replied, "Don't urge me to leave you or to turn back from you. Where you go I will go, and where you stay I will stay. Your people will be my people and your God my God. Where you die I will die, and there I will be buried. May the LORD deal with me, be it ever so severely, if anything but death separates you and me." When Naomi realized that Ruth was*

51

determined to go with her, she stopped urging her.

When we look at these verses closely, a process of true covenant relationship is revealed:

1. Decision—*Don't urge me to leave you or ...*

2. Submission—*...to turn back from you.*

3. Commitment—*Where you go I will go ...*

4. Friendship—*...where you stay I will stay.*

5. Oneness—*Your people will be my people...*

6. Spiritual unity—*... and your God my God.*

7. Determination—*Where you die I will die;*

8. Paying the price—*there I will be buried.*

9. Lasting Fellowship—*May the LORD deal with me ...*

10. Covenant relationship—*... if anything but death parts us.*

The third challenge is that of *washing the feet of our covenant friend.* That means focusing on the process of making our friend a qualified leader by cleansing and purifying. *When the Lord gives us a covenant and faithful friend in personal life, ministry, or business, it is—as we discussed earlier—a two-way street.*

52

They support and encourage us; we develop and build them up.

This process of washing feet—cleansing and purifying—involves intentional actions that:

- Affirm your covenant relationship—anything from praying to taking time for a cup of coffee to, yes, physically washing their feet.

- Cleanse and purify the person or their growth process. This might include clarifying some point of the person's developmental process, or offering advice or correction with the clear intent of advancing your covenant friend.

- Take this friend to your mountain of glory as well as your mountain of agony. Be transparent with your true successes and failures, fears, disappointments, personal struggles, challenges, and problems.

Who is John for you in business, ministry, private life, public life, and as a leader? How many people like John do you have? What has been your contribution to their lives? When is the last time John was actually surprised when you washed his feet in humility and covenant relationship?

My own mother filled this role for me when she was alive. After I graduated with my doctorate from Michigan State University, I traveled back to my parent's home in my village in Ethiopia with the specific mission of washing my mother's and father's feet.

My parents were very happy about my earning a PhD. It was something far beyond their dreams. We had a wonderful reunion, and then I told my parents about my desire to wash their feet. As the last child, washing my parents' feet was my responsibility as I grew up. This time, because of my formal education, my mother refused at first. She said I didn't need to do any such thing. But I gently persuaded her and my father that it was truly something I wanted to do. I reminded them that I was still their last child.

In the end, they allowed me the great privilege of washing their feet to honor them. This was a very special event, as God would have it. It was the last time I saw my mother.

I still carry that precious memory with me.

Chapter Six

WASHING PETER'S FEET

H e came to Simon Peter, who said to him, "Lord, are you going to wash my feet?" Jesus replied, "You do not realize now what I am doing, but later you will understand." "No," said Peter, "you shall never wash my feet." Jesus answered, "Unless I wash you, you have no part with me." "Then, Lord," Simon Peter replied, "not just my feet but my hands and my head as well!" (John 13:6-9)*

WHO IS PETER FOR JESUS?

Peter, too, was a successful fisherman. A business partner of the sons of Zebedee (Luke 5:10), Peter was encouraged by his brother Andrew to listen to Jesus' call to become a disciple (John 1:40-42). Peter was a bold individual, full of enthusiasm. He sometimes spoke and acted before thinking. For example, Peter was first among the disciples to identify Jesus as the Christ (Mark 8:27-30). Yet moments later, Peter was telling Jesus that he knew more about Jesus' messianic task than did Jesus Himself (Mark 8:31, 32). When Jesus corrected Peter with the phrase *"Get behind me, Satan!"* (Mark 8:33), however, it wasn't about correcting Peter's understanding of the Messiah's task. It was because Jesus heard the voice of the tempter in Peter encouraging Him to avoid Jerusalem and the cross.

Peter is a friend who gives advice for almost everything. Such friends think that they know what is good for you. Usually they are more concerned about your wellbeing than about your destiny. The enemy may use their good intentions to distract you from your destiny. Their motive is good, but they lack discernment.

Peter was impatient. He needed clarity to move ahead. He wasn't afraid to ask questions to understand something better. And once Peter understood something, he would strive to fulfill it even if it required an extra measure of faith on his part. Remember, Peter was the disciple who asked Jesus if he could walk on water with Him (Matthew 14:22-33), even if only for a few steps. Peter didn't finish what he started because he was afraid. His fear began when he started looking at his environment. The same thing happened to him when he denied Jesus. He started out well by telling Jesus he would never deny him, but when he looked at his surroundings in Herod's courtyard, fear over took him again.

Peter was also remarkably insecure from time to time. His mood swings were evident even at the time of his calling (Luke 5:4-11), where he began with the attitude of a confident veteran fisherman, became humiliated to the point of shame, and then became a willing follower of Jesus.

His fear and, perhaps again, shame were evident in the incident when he denied Jesus in the courtyard of the high priest (Luke 22:55-62). Two witnesses claimed they saw him with Jesus. Peter denied their assertions. Yet a third man apparently used Peter's Galilean accent to connect him with Jesus. In Jerusalem, Galileans were treated like remote rural folk in our day. The assumption was that Galileans were uncultured, uneducated folk who couldn't speak well. The shame that overwhelmed Peter at the moment the rooster crowed must have been excruciating. No matter what his real feeling toward Jesus, he had denied Him three times. He was reminded of the cultural

57

shame of being a Galilean, and aware of his own shame as a disloyal friend.

Yet one who denies you can become one who ultimately gives up his life for you. Jesus restored Peter into a relationship with Him, and into leadership with His people, with the simple command, "Feed my sheep"—and the renewed invitation to "Follow me!" (John 21). Pentecost marked a new day for the big fisherman as a key leader in the early church (Acts 2), and perhaps with the recognition that among many tongues a Galilean accent didn't stand out any more than others. Peter learned to forgive himself as Jesus had forgiven him. Then he was free to accept his destiny as a leader in the first century church.

Jesus frequently dealt with Peter's quick temper and rash conclusions. The Lord recognized Peter's tendency to express the easy way out, whether it was to stay on the Mount of Transfiguration or for Jesus to try an easier road to fulfill His messianic mission. Yet for all Peter's faults, it was easy for Jesus to recognize his potential. Peter was a man of great faith and belief. He was an able student of Jesus. He wanted

58

desperately to grow in his understanding of the Lord and His ways.

WHO IS PETER FOR YOU?

Peter represents a diamond in the rough that may frustrate you today but bring you great returns in the future, if you invest in him the right kind of encouragement and formation. He sometimes covers his insecurities with great statements of valor. He longs to prove himself worthy by overcoming his upbringing with a noble act or great words. He is often an overachiever.

Peter is given to you so that you may give him a name of destiny. When Andrew, Peter's brother, brought him to Jesus, *Jesus looked at him and said, "You are Simon son of John. You shall be called Cephas— which translated is Peter [Stone]"* (John 1:42 AMP). From that day, the Lord Jesus treated him not as Simon, but as Peter because of his potential. Jesus trained him and prayed for him and told him to encourage his brothers when he went back. Jesus forgave Peter even before he denied Him. Peter provides the leader with a school of forgiveness and restoration, as both will be necessary to mature him well.

Who is Peter for you? Watch for these characteristics in the people around you:

- Someone showing great, yet unpolished, leadership potential;

- Someone who desires to do his best time and time again in an effort to overcome what he perceives to be a faulty background;

- Someone who will adventure with you into uncharted areas;

- Someone who seeks to find the easiest, if not always the best, path;

- Someone who looks for your input and encouragement.

WASHING PETER'S FEET

It is not always easy to wash Peter's feet.

It was certainly never easy to wash my uncle's feet, either. He was big and bombastic, just as I imagine Peter to have been. He was an annual visitor to our home in the outlands of Ethiopia. You would never know we were related. In fact, many times I tried to convince myself there was no way this man was my uncle. He was huge. I was tiny, especially in the years I was still at home. His feet

60

were about the length of my arm from the elbow to my fingertips. To make matters worse, his feet didn't even fit in my family's wash basin.

As the youngest child, it was my responsibility to wash the feet of our guests—especially relatives. My uncle was no exception. But for all the times I tried to wash his feet, I just couldn't seem to do it to his standards. I never had enough water in the basin. I didn't wash his feet hard enough one time, or gently enough the next. The towel was too damp or too scratchy. But it was my task, my duty, so I completed it nonetheless.

Peter's weaknesses did not stop Jesus from washing Peter's feet, either.

When Jesus turned to Peter to wash his feet, He knew Peter would deny knowing Him three times that night. Peter had no idea of what would take place. The New Testament call is to serve those like Peter.

Once again, Peter found himself trying to correct Jesus about protocol. Earlier the correction had been about how Jesus defined his mission as the Messiah. On this Thursday night, Peter seemed to feel he had the right to negotiate how and when Jesus washed feet.

One commentary postulates: "Possibly the same pride [among the disciples] had expressed itself on this same evening in a controversy about places at table. Jesus, conscious of His divine dignity and against Peter's protest, performed for them this lowliest service. His act of humility actually cleansed their hearts of selfish ambition, killed their pride, and taught them the lesson of love."[3]

One challenge in washing a Peter's feet is to *not give up on the person in whom you see potential; however they act in the process.* The ones who are Peters in our lives are there to teach us forgiveness and restoration.

A second challenge is *to help the person forgive himself when necessary so he can take another step toward his destiny.* In God's Kingdom, one's mistakes are not meant to be served up cold as a reminder of failure. Even in saying "Get behind me, Satan," Jesus was careful to separate the potential from the personality. Jesus was well aware Peter would make mistakes. The key was to remind Peter that he was destined to be The Rock.

Third, we must face the challenge of *exercising trust based not upon today, but tomorrow.* We must remind Peter again and again of the potential we see in him. This is another failure of many leaders today. We believe that if we err on the side of too much encouragement, those we lead will swell up in pride. Frankly, after three decades in international and public ministry, I have yet to see that happen. Remember that Jesus Himself found it a challenge to build Peter back to the point where the fisherman would even begin to let go of his past, including his failures, and move into His future.

This is a demanding process for the leader. It requires an ability to see potential in people, then name the person with potential, and then develop that person. Such development is usually not subtle, because most people like Peter won't process subtleties very well.

The beauty of developing the Peter people around us is that you will see the change and growth from the first time they agree to follow without considering the cost (Matthew 4), and when they agree to follow having begun to count the cost (John 21).

The difference is worth the process.

"He who loves a pure heart and whose speech is gracious will have the king for his friend."
Proverbs 22:11

Chapter Seven

WASHING THOMAS' FEET

Now Thomas (called Didymus), one of the Twelve, was not with the disciples when Jesus came. So the other disciples told him, "We have seen the Lord!" But he said to them, "Unless I see the nail marks in his hands and put my finger where the nails were, and put my hand into his side, I will not believe it." A week later his disciples were in the house again, and Thomas was with them. Though the doors were locked, Jesus came and stood among them and said, "Peace be with you!" Then he said to Thomas, "Put your finger here; see my hands. Reach out your hand and put it into my side. Stop doubting and believe." Thomas said to him, "My Lord and my God!" (John 20:24-28)

WHO IS THOMAS FOR JESUS?

When you mention the name "Thomas" among the disciples, the first response for many is, "That's 'Doubting Thomas,' isn't it?" Indeed, Thomas is known for his doubts. His character did not tolerate symbolic illustrations or fluffy language well. But that was not necessarily because he was cynical about Jesus' teaching. Instead, Thomas was the one disciple who would ask questions when the others were too embarrassed to open their mouths.

On the night Jesus washed the disciples' feet, He also said He was going away to His Father's house. He told the disciples that they knew the way there (John 14:4). Thomas couldn't let that pass. What was Jesus talking about? He and the other disciples had no clue where Jesus was going. In fact, just hearing about it frightened them. So Thomas made the issue clear for everyone involved: *"Lord, we don't know where you are going, so how can we know the way?"* (John 14:5). Very practical and to the point, Thomas wanted the issue broken down so anyone around that table could understand it.

Indeed, Thomas' reputation was of one who challenged everything. Thomas was not one to take anything at face value. He needed his own "integrity check" to know whether something deserved his attention, much less his devotion. That said, Thomas knew that Jesus had profound integrity by the time the news came that Lazarus had fallen seriously ill. After two days, Jesus told the disciples it was time to travel back to Judea to "wake up" Lazarus, who had already died. The disciples reminded Jesus that on their last visit to Judea some Jews had tried to stone Jesus. It was a dangerous place, but Jesus was determined to help their friend Lazarus. Thomas spoke up to the other disciples, *"Let us also go, that we may die with [Jesus]"* (John 11:1-16). However many challenges Thomas threw Jesus' way, once Thomas had seen Jesus' integrity, he was willing to follow with absolute loyalty.

Thomas represents a person who demands integrity. He is given to us for a reality check, especially for those of us who tend to work only in the "big picture" without giving a second thought to details. Thomas is the one who says, "Don't *tell* me your vision, *show* me. What's your strategy? Give me evidence. Show me you're a great husband, wife, father, mother, or leader. Have you done this before?"

It's easy to become frustrated with Thomas, but we must remember that Thomas said "Show me!" even to Jesus (John 20:24-28). Say what you will, careful reflection will reveal that no one among the disciples wanted to believe more than Thomas. When Jesus was crucified, Thomas was probably among those who hurt most. He had found a reason to believe in Jesus, and couldn't understand what happened to his Teacher. Thomas had overcome his cynicism and believed, only to have that belief and trust shattered on Golgotha. So Thomas set his standards: *"Unless I see the nail marks in his hands and put my finger where the nails were, and put my hand into his side, I will not believe [Jesus had risen]"* (John 20:25). A week later, the resurrected Jesus gave Thomas that very opportunity.

Over time, I have come to appreciate Thomas more and more. Why? The disciples were sitting in a room, post-resurrection, when Jesus entered the room. He breathed the Holy Spirit into them, and they stayed in the closed room. They told Thomas what happened. He probably thought, "If that's true, what are you doing here in a closed room?" Fear caused them to close the door on God's power and opportunity to witness. When Jesus welcomed Thomas' touch, Thomas' response was "My Lord and my God!"—and the Gospel was well on its way to the public again.

I once had an assistant who asked detailed questions about everything I did, including my travel receipts. She would even question why I

68

needed two coffees in one day. At first, I resented this kind of question. A coffee to begin the day and another to keep me awake during an early evening layover later in the day didn't seem too lavish to me. Why should I be questioned about such a thing?

Then I realized that my assistant was actually questioning me to protect my integrity. It looked odd to her, and rightly so, that I would turn in receipts from Ethiopia that seemed to be dated eight years behind the dates of my travel. But the explanation was simple. If the business ran by the Ethiopian calendar, the receipt would indeed appear to be eight years behind because the Ethiopian calendar is eight years behind the calendars in the rest of the world. Once I sat down with my assistant and looked at a current Ethiopian calendar to verify that fact, the issue was resolved.

WHO IS THOMAS FOR YOU?

Who is Thomas for you? God puts Thomas in our lives to challenge us to ever-greater integrity. He is the reality check so many visionary leaders need on their teams. Look for:

- Someone who will not commit unless they sense integrity in a leader or a project;

- Someone who demands evidence or proof before moving ahead;

- A person who, once given the evidence desired, fully throws himself into a cause or project;

- Someone who is not afraid to ask questions;

- Someone who rarely takes anything at face value.

WASHING THOMAS' FEET

Thomas not only conveyed skepticism about Jesus' teaching, he doubted Christ's resurrection from the dead when others told him it was true. Yet Jesus, knowing Thomas' questioning nature, did not complain about Thomas' unbelief. Instead Jesus washed Thomas' feet, treating Thomas like a hero of faith. Jesus knew Thomas was going to challenge everything. Yet Jesus washed his feet. That's biblical leadership.

The frustration we have with Thomas is that he won't trust us at face value. Yet God gives us Thomas as a balance, as God's reality check. Visionary leaders have the dream; Thomas demands the reality to make it happen.

The first challenge in washing Thomas' feet is to *treat his challenges as necessary "reality checks" for, rather than threats against, your vision.* When Thomas people know their challenges have been taken seriously and even acted upon, their trust level increases. You benefit from taking seriously reasonable challenges to your vision, as well. God puts checks and balances in your life for a reason.

The second Thomas challenge is to *bring evidence to support your vision, claims, or projects.* The Thomas in your life will probably respond well to facts, figures, and case studies. Let him see models, examples, perhaps even newspaper articles, or Scriptural evidence, if it's appropriate.

The third challenge is not unique to reaching the Thomas in your life, but still very important to that individual: *Support what you say with character that matches or exceeds your words.* Who you are in Christ is more important than what you say about Him. The Thomas people in your life notice actions first, and words second.

Remember, God brings Thomases into our lives to provide reality checks for all we do. Nurture your relationships with them through regular footwashing events. Invite their constructive criticisms into your leadership process, and you'll both be blessed.

Chapter Eight

WASHING THE OTHER DISCIPLES' FEET

esus went on to say, "This is why I told you that **J** *noman can come to me unless the Father has enabled him." From this time many of his disciples turned back and no longer followed him.* (John 6:65-66)

At first his disciples did not understand all this [fulfillment of prophecy surrounding Jesus' triumphal entry into Jerusalem]. Only after Jesus was glorified did they realize that these things had been written about him and that they had done these things to him. (John 12:16)

To the Jews who believed him, Jesus said, "If you hold to my teaching, you are really my disciples. Then you will know the truth, and the truth will set you free." (John 8:31)

WHO ARE THE OTHERS FOR JESUS?

If someone were making up the stories in the Bible, don't you think they would have cleaned up the parts that made the disciples look bad? Very often, the Twelve and the others who followed Jesus didn't have a clue about what was going on before their very eyes—and Who was behind it.

The people of Palestine in the day of Jesus were desperate for the return of the Messiah. The Romans had destroyed their Temple and were an uncomfortable fit at best as an occupying force. The Jews were more than ready for the Messiah to drive out the Roman intruders by force and shame. Many who had followed Jesus were counting on Him to come as a political ruler. They really didn't understand Jesus' mission and purpose, especially when His mission and purpose conflicted with their own messianic expectations. The Scriptures are clear about the results of these growing value conflicts. As Jesus' ministry continued, His disciples fell victim to fear, disappointment, and confusion (John 6:65-66).

Make no mistake, however. Even the disciples who remained background characters in the Gospels were part of the powerful force that went out in pairs to heal the sick, cast out demons, and preach the Gospel (Luke 10:1-24). They knew they were part of something big, but rarely, if ever, did they

74

understand just how big the "something" was (John 12:16).

Mostly, they didn't believe what Jesus had been teaching them for three years. Crucifixion? Resurrection? Unheard of. What do you say to those who only hear what they want to hear? They already have their own paradigm, and that's what they're pushing for: their value system, not the King's.

So when Jesus was actually taken away to be tried and crucified, they were shattered. They ran away and went into hiding.

Individuals might be with you when things go smoothly because they anticipate self-gratification. Clearly, some of the disciples as we see them in the Gospels used Jesus to buttress their own status rather than being used of the Lord. Jesus was part of their personal ladder to success. Then they scattered under pressure, as will such individuals in your life.

The other disciples are still in limbo regarding their commitment. They still have to sort out what it means to be a follower. God brings the other disciples into our lives to teach us not to depend upon flesh and blood. When they leave you, they

75

will teach you about your response when everything seems to turn sour.

Like it or not, these are the majority of your followers. Having said that, don't lose heart. People like John, Peter, and Thomas will emerge from this group over time. The truth of the matter is, you don't completely know who you're nurturing among this number.

Again, Jesus' example provides wisdom on how to work with this group. Consider the two disciples on the road to Emmaus (Luke 24:13-35). Jesus asked them, "Why are you so discouraged?" They explained their version of Jesus' trial, crucifixion, and resurrection, all of which indicated that they felt Jesus' mission had been a failure. Jesus then gave them a thorough explanation of what had happened, setting their hearts afire for the first time in days.

It would have certainly been fair for Jesus to ask, "How about all I did for these guys? Does that account for anything?" But their paradigm was still an obstacle to seeing the true mission of the Messiah. They decided not to wait in Jerusalem for the promised Holy Spirit. They thought it was over. Discouragement and disappointment took over.

When Jesus drew near to walk with them, their faces were downcast. Jesus could see the depth of their hopelessness in their physical appearance. In the end, what Jesus had done for these disciples wasn't important to them until He explained, in detail, what was going on around them.

WHO ARE THE OTHER DISCIPLES FOR YOU?

Who are the other disciples for you? Watch for:

- Those who follow you but don't understand the "big picture" issues that drive you;

- Those who are still deciding about their commitment level to you;

- Those who may not understand why they do what they do in the context of your organization or relationship;

- Those who are confused or even discouraged about their place in your cause.

Remember, a leader may ask "How about all I did for these guys?" when these other disciples seem ready to walk away. What you did doesn't matter at that moment. The first key is understanding what God is doing for you as you feel deserted by the flesh and blood around you. The second key is your ability to leave an open door for them so that when they decide to labor alongside you, they will have a place in the Kingdom work. The third key is to walk with them until their eyes are opened to reality and they return to the original calling. Jesus successfully did these things for the disciples on Emmaus road by:

- Taking time to walk with them on the road;

- Asking soul-searing questions;

- Sharing revelation with them that brought back fire and passion they lost;

- Continuing to lead until they asked Him to come in and spent the night with them.

- Breaking bread with them in fellowship that opened their eyes;

- Giving them understanding of the Scriptures. Once they received the fire (open heart), revelation of who He was (open eyes) and understood the truth (open mind), they went back to Jerusalem to wait for the promised Holy Spirit.

WASHING THE OTHER DISCIPLES' FEET

Jesus washed the feet of the disciples who were about to abandon Him in His time of deepest despair. They indicated they would not leave or abandon Jesus when He was arrested, but they did. Yet Jesus did not complain about what He knew was coming. Instead Jesus washed their feet, treating them as His faithful friends. In fact, He told those who came to arrest Him to let His disciples go, since the soldiers were looking for Him. Why did He do this?

Because *New Testament ministry does not depend upon the ups and downs of those who are served, but the relationship the servant maintains with the Lord.* God only uses a person who is ready to wash everyone's feet, without prejudice or discrimination. Clearly, we need to follow Jesus' example of relational leadership.

So the first challenge in washing the feet of this group is to *look past their own insecurities, toward their futures.* Here, you may not have the kind of clear indications of a potential Peter or Thomas or John in every person. You simply honor the fact that God has a future and a hope for them that, somehow, you are meant to nurture.

The second challenge is to *explain time and again what you are doing and their part in it*. This allows you to correct the paradigms they brought with them into their relationship with you and your organization. Remember that this need not be a formal teaching session. In fact, it is often better as informal instruction.

The third challenge for a leader who seeks to wash the feet of this group is to *exercise great patience in helping people in this group advance through your investment in time, education, and equipping*. Once again, this is not the time to ask, "How about all I've done for these guys?" Instead, you have a prime opportunity to grow as a leader. Some successes can be measured on a timeline; however, true biblical leadership impact can only be measured in the light of God's purposes and eternity. Everything that can't be measured on a scale is not an indication of failure.

Disciples can be committed one day and fearful, discouraged, confused, and hopeless the next. The key for the footwashing leader is to do those things that continue to purify, cleanse, and clarify the path of these other disciples. Some of them will be transformed into leaders ready to show others how to advance in life and the Kingdom.

_____

*"Create in me a pure heart, O God, and renew a
steadfast spirit within me."*
Psalm 51:10

Chapter Nine

WASHING JUDAS ISCARIOT'S FEET

S ix days before the Passover, Jesus arrived at Bethany, where Lazarus lived, whom Jesus had raised from the dead. Here a dinner was given in Jesus' honor. Martha served, while Lazarus was among those reclining at the table with him. Then Mary took about a pint of pure nard, an expensive perfume; she poured it on Jesus' feet and wiped his feet with her hair. And the house was filled with the fragrance of perfume.

But one of the disciples, Judas Iscariot, who was later to betray him, objected, "Why wasn't this perfume sold and the money given to the poor? It was worth a year's wages!" He did not say this because he cared about the poor but because he was a thief; as keeper of the money bag, he used to help himself to what was in the money bag.

"Leave her alone," Jesus replied. "It was intended that she should save this perfume for the day of my burial.

You will always have the poor among you, but you will not always have me." (John 12:1-8)

WHO IS JUDAS ISCARIOT FOR JESUS?

The Bible is pretty tough on Judas Iscariot, and for good reason. It isn't everyone whose name goes down in history as a synonym for "traitor."

Much speculation surrounds the meaning of the word "Iscariot." Some scholars attach a dark meaning like "dagger-bearer" or "man of the lie" to the word. Others simply assign a tribal or geographic meaning like "man of Issachar" or "man of Kerioth," which could have made him the only non-Galilean among the disciples. If that was an issue, Judas might have spent his whole stint as a disciple feeling slighted.

We can assume from the Scriptures that Judas Iscariot was present for Jesus' miracles. He was almost certainly present for most of Jesus' teaching. It might be troubling to think about, but as best we can tell, Judas was a member of the two-by-two ministry teams that had great success in healing, deliverance, and teaching ministry.

So what went wrong? Simply put, we don't know. It seems evident from his continued pilfering from the treasury that Judas didn't let the Gospel take root in his heart (John 12:6). Clearly, Jesus knew the character of Judas early on in His ministry (John 6:70, 71).

In the big picture, Judas just wasn't satisfied with Jesus' leadership. At the end of the day, Judas was willing to do what it took to take Jesus out of the picture—for a profit (Matthew 26:14-16).

Judas is a tough one to figure out. He was among the disciples, yet never really on the team. The love of money clearly distracted him. He seemed to show no growth in integrity or moral fiber. The tone of the gospel writers clearly indicates their irritation with Judas on one hand, and the disciples' relative cluelessness about him on the other. Judas takes ruthless action against Jesus on one hand, and on the other hand, feels remorse when it's too late to do anything about it.

Judas represents the person in your life who will assist you in the process of dying to self through actions that others—and probably you, too—will perceive as being traitorous and detestable. Judas is not about helping you and your team along in the

85

process; he is simply about the business of crucifying you—even crucifixion by memo. He will bring you into the final and culminating stage of leadership, where you must be crucified with Christ.

WHO IS JUDAS FOR YOU?

Who is Judas for you? This is a difficult issue that must be considered with the utmost care. Unlike Jesus' Judas, your Judas may still repent. This is why washing the feet of Judas is so important in this generation. Look for the following traits in those who surround you:

- Someone obsessed with self-benefit;

- Someone who seems to be consistently dishonest;

- Someone who remains on the fringe of your ministry or organization;

- Someone who constantly and openly questions the motives of others;

- Someone who can "talk the right language" but only infrequently aligns his or her behavior with it.

WASHING JUDAS ISCARIOT'S FEET

At the very moment Jesus washed his feet, Judas was waiting for a suitable time to hand Jesus over to the enemy (Matthew 26:16). Because leadership or ministry is not primarily a reflection of the people you serve, but rather a reflection of who you are, Jesus also washed the feet of the one who was going to betray him.

It is beyond human imagination to expect anyone to wash the feet of a person he knows will hand him over to the foe. But Jesus, knowing Judas was influenced by evil and the love of money, knelt down before him and washed his feet! Jesus dried Judas' feet just as He did for the others. What Jesus did for Judas was not a reflection of Judas, but was a reflection of Himself. This is a prime example of how authority and love are tied together. Jesus said He loved Peter, Thomas, the others, and Judas to the end. There's no break from love. You can take a vacation from work, but you can't take a vacation from loving those God has given you to lead—no matter how they treat you.

A remarkable man of God is pastoring a unique church in Rwanda as I write this. This pastor watched in horror from under a tree just outside his rural Rwandan village as his family was slaughtered by a group of people who for years had been his neighbors. For years following that tragic day, God worked in that pastor's heart to keep him strong as he grieved. As for many Rwandans, it was difficult for him to hear that almost all of those who had killed his family and friends were pardoned as part of the reconciliation movement within the country.

Then the man heard a clear call from God: "Pastor the people who killed those you loved." Obviously, this was not an easy call to accept. Yet he obeyed God's call. As he told me not long ago, "Now I am pastoring those who took everything and everyone I knew from me. And I am pastoring them not because of me, but of God."

Judas is certainly one of the most, if not the most, demanding person whose feet we are called to wash. Indeed, the first challenge in washing Judas' feet is to *continue to serve, without prejudice, the one who seems determined to harm you.* This is a key stage in dying to self. It is important to put this into practice; in so doing you are giving your behavior to the Lord and His control rather than allowing your personal Judas to control it.

The second challenge is, as much as possible, *to limit or eliminate opportunities that might trigger hostility in the one who would harm you.* It is true that Judas' behavior may often be erratic and hostile no matter what you do. Yet it is wise not to provide needless opportunity for his negative behavior to emerge.

The final challenge is to *continue to provide Judas opportunities to show responsibility and teamwork.* Jesus did this for Judas Iscariot. That Judas was a visible failure among his peers. Your Judas might actually respond, perhaps after some time, in positive ways to these opportunities.

Remember that, all in all, *Judas is on your team not to support you, but to crucify you.* He is almost entirely obsessed with his own benefit. Judas can "talk the talk" of charity and self-sacrifice, but his actions rarely lines up with his words. Judas is waiting for the right time to take you out at the knees. Judas may kiss you, but not everyone who kisses you is motivated by love and respect.

There is no way to serve Judas until you die to yourself. This must be truth in your life: that you have been crucified with Christ, and that it is no longer you who live, but Christ that lives in you. Christ in you will wash the feet of Judas. Love him.

Forgive him, even if he never repents. Pass your final test of leadership.

Chapter Ten

THE FOOTWASHING PROJECT

THE SEVEN DAY CHALLENGE

TO DEVELOP A SERVANT'S HEART

*hen [Jesus] had finished washing their feet, he put on his clothes and returned to his place. "Do you understand what I have done for you?" he asked them. "You call me 'Teacher' and 'Lord,' and rightly so, for that is what I am. Now that I, your Lord and Teacher, have washed your feet, you also should wash one another's feet. I have set you an example that you should do as I have done for you. I tell you the truth, no servant is greater than his master, nor is a messenger greater than the one who sent him. **Now that you know these things, you will be blessed if you do them.**"* (John 13:12-17)

THE PRACTICAL SIDE OF WASHING FEET

I can tell you from practical and personal experience that there is nothing glamorous about washing feet. You can wash a feet of someone either because of obligation (as I did for my uncle) or true and sincere love (as I did for my parents).

Truly, washing feet shows where the blessedness of the servant lies. Satisfaction in one's ministry does not come from the type of gift one receives from God, or what one does to succeed, or even what is accomplished. Satisfaction comes from one's ability and readiness to serve others. *"Now that you know all these things, you will be blessed if you do them."*(John 13:17) The blessing is not in receiving authority, but in faithfully submitting ourselves to God and others in response to the authority God has given us. It is difficult for our human minds to imagine giving up the trappings of high position to give ourselves to service. Still, the blessing lies not only in knowing the truth—but in living it.

The Path for Lasting Blessings of the Kingdom: Complete the Seven-Day Footwashing Cycle— Through a prayer focus for each day for a week and continue making this your life style.

Throughout this book, we have examined the relational side of footwashing, and how vital the discipline of this "relational footwashing" is. But why should we take the time and effort to follow through? Let's answer that question with this question: What are you consistently doing to affirm your commitment to those around you? Jesus proved His commitment to those in His everyday life on earth by taking the role of the footwasher, whether or not a physical towel and basin were on hand.

Using our spiritual gifts to serve others with unconditional love and humility reflects our relationship with the Lord. It demonstrates the focus and purpose of our calling—and defines the core of true spiritual service and biblical leadership.

Toward that end, here is a seven-day plan to develop a servant's heart and secure unconditional blessings through footwashing. We begin with demonstrating our devotion to the Lord by washing His feet in worship as did Mary at Bethany (John 12:1-8), and continue in gratitude as we serve those Jesus has given us.

Indeed, gratitude is the basis for launching and continuing this discipline of footwashing. Think of the account of Jesus' feet being washed: the "sinful woman" who anointed Jesus' feet at the home of Simon the Pharisee (Luke 7:36-50). Simon was ready to condemn both the woman and Jesus. Jesus took the opportunity to challenge Simon with the truth that what the woman lacked in decorum, Simon lacked in love and simple gratitude that Jesus visited his home.

How grateful to God are you? If you are truly grateful to God, your gratitude—like that of the sinful woman—will overflow in humble, footwashing service to others.

The seven-day footwashing cycle presented below will lead you in bowing your knee and your heart to the Lord and to those whom God has given you to lead.

"The goal of this command is love,
which comes from a pure hear
and a good conscience and a sincere faith."
1Timothy 1:5

DAY ONE: SUNDAY

I. FOCUS: Wash the feet of the Risen Lord with worship and praises.

II. PERSON TO REMEMBER: The Lord God.

III. PRACTICAL THING TO DO: An act that honors God (describe it here):

1. What will you do to honor the Lord in a very special way this week? _____

_____

_____

2. What will you adjust in your lifestyle to honor the Lord the rest of your life? _____

_____

_____

IV. PRAYER APPROPRIATE FOR TODAY: Speak your desire to submit your glory to the Lord, as did Mary when she washed Jesus' feet with her hair.

1. **Scripture:** *Six days before the Passover, Jesus arrived at Bethany, where Lazarus lived, whom Jesus had raised from the dead. Here a dinner was given in Jesus' honor. Martha served, while Lazarus was among those reclining at the table with him. Then Mary took about a pint of pure nard, an expensive perfume; she poured it on Jesus' feet and wiped his feet with her hair. And the house was filled with the fragrance of perfume.* (John 12:1-3)

2. **Reflection:** Wash the feet of the Lord with true worship. Pour the perfume on His feet as did Mary. Give Him your best. Wipe His feet with your hair. Put your glory under His feet. Show Him your true love and affection with all your heart, soul, mind, and strength. Repeat this every day as many times as possible.

V.   LIST YOUR PRAISES:

1.   _____

2.   _____

3.   _____

4. _____

5. _____

VI. WRITE WHAT THE LORD IS SAYING TO YOU AND YOUR RESPONSE TO HIM:

1. _____

2. _____

3. _____

4. _____

5. _____

DAY TWO: MONDAY

I. FOCUS: Wash the feet of your immediate family.

II. PEOPLE TO REMEMBER: Each of your family members, with special focus on the one with whom you need to become closer today.

III. PRACTICAL THING TO DO: Any act that demonstrates your heart to serve your family members (describe it here):

1. _____

2. _____

3. _____

4. _____

5. _____

IV. PRAYER APPROPRIATE FOR TODAY: Bless your family in spoken prayer, taking the time needed to be specific with each family member.

1. **Scripture:** *Submit to one another out of reverence for Christ. Wives, submit to your husbands as to the Lord ...Husbands, love your wives as Christ loved the church and gave himself up for her....Children, obey your parents in the Lord, for this is right. "Honor your father and mother"... Fathers, do not exasperate your children; instead, bring them up in the training and instruction of the Lord.* (Ephesians 5:21, 22, 25, 6:1, 2, 4)

2. **Reflection:** Take time today to express your true love and care to your spouse and children. Pray for each member of your family, and make time to do or discuss something special with your spouse and children today, even if it is simply a few moments on the telephone. *The man said, "This is now bone of my bone and flesh of my flesh..."* (Genesis 2:23) is an expression of washing a spouse's feet. Say things that are edifying, encouraging, and uplifting as a priest of your home. Declare and decree the purpose of God and His blessings over them as you bless them.

V. LIST PRACTICAL STEPS YOU SHOULD TAKE TO BE A BETTER PRIEST OF YOUR HOME:

1. _____

2. _____

3. _____

4. _____

5. _____

DAY THREE: TUESDAY

I.   FOCUS: Wash the feet of Johns—people of covenant in your life.

II. PERSON TO IDENTIFY: Whoever has functioned as John for you this week (see Chapter 5).

III. PRACTICAL THING TO DO: An act that reinforces your relationship with "John" (describe it here):

   1. Who are the covenant people in your life?

      ➢ _____

      ➢ _____

      ➢ _____

      ➢ _____

      ➢ _____

   2. What do you need to do to strengthen your covenant?

      ➢ _____

      ➢ _____

      ➢ _____

102

➤ _____

➤ _____

IV. PRAYER APPROPRIATE FOR TODAY: Pray that you will offer John the example and specific help needed to fully develop her/his potential.

1. **Scripture:** *Near the cross of Jesus stood his mother, his mother's sister, Mary the wife of Clopas, and Mary Magdalene. When Jesus saw his mother there, and the disciple whom he loved standing nearby, he said to his mother, "Dear woman, here is your son," and to the disciple, "Here is your mother." From that time on, this disciple took her into his home.* (John 19:25-27)

2. **Reflection:** Take time today to support your covenant friend in prayer and find a few moments to encourage your friend over the phone, via e-mail, or face-to-face over coffee. Thank your friend for being trustworthy and sensitive to your wellbeing. WHAT IS THE LORD SAYING TO YOU ABOUT COVENANT RELATIONSHIP?

➤ _____

➤ _____

➢ _____

➢ _____

➢ _____

DAY FOUR: WEDNESDAY

I.   FOCUS: Wash the feet of Peter.

II. PERSON TO IDENTIFY: The person who functions as Peter for you (see Chapter 6).

III. PRACTICAL THING TO DO: Pointing out a specific skill of "Peter's" that helps you (describe it here):

_____

_____

IV. PRAYER APPROPRIATE FOR TODAY: Ask to see Peter through God's eyes, especially to see his/her gifts and talents. Thank God for them.

   1. **Scripture:** *He came to Simon Peter, who said to him, "Lord, are you going to wash my feet?" Jesus replied, "You do not realize now what I am doing, but later you will understand." No," said Peter, "you shall never wash my feet." Jesus answered, "Unless I wash you, you have no part with me." "Then, Lord," Simon Peter replied,*

"not just my feet but my hands and my head as well!" (John 13:6-9)

2. **Reflection:** Pray that you will find ways to nurture Peter both as a person and as a potential leader. Pray specifically that Peter will become more secure in his role now and develop greater leadership skills this week. If you can name those skills to bless him/her specifically, all the better. People like Peter thrive on one-on-one attention, too. Use this time to check your heart about walking in forgiveness. Give the Lord permission to search your heart (Psalm 139:24).

V. LIST PETERS IN YOUR LIFE:

1. _____

2. _____

3. _____

4. _____

5. _____

V.   WHAT ACTION ARE YOU ARE YOU GOING TO TAKE THAT WILL SHOW YOUR UNCONDITIONAL LOVE AND FORGIVENESS OF THESE INDIVIDUALS?

1. _____

2. _____

3. _____

4. _____

5. _____

DAY FIVE: THURSDAY

I. FOCUS: Wash the feet of Thomas.

II. PERSON TO IDENTIFY: The person who functions
    as Thomas for you (see Chapter 7).

III. PRACTICAL THING TO DO: Ask Thomas to review
     your organization or your leadership.

IV. PRAYER APPROPRIATE FOR TODAY: Thank God for
    Thomas' desire for complete integrity; pray
    that his/her "integrity checking" will not
    become legalistic.

    1. **Scripture:** *Now Thomas (called Didymus), one
        of the Twelve, was not with the disciples when
        Jesus came. So the other disciples told him, "We
        have seen the Lord!" But he said to them,
        "Unless I see the nail marks in his hands and
        put my finger where the nails were, and put my
        hand into his side, I will not believe it." A week
        later his disciples were in the house again, and
        Thomas was with them. Though the doors were*

locked, Jesus came and stood among them and said, "Peace be with you!" Then he said to Thomas, "Put your finger here; see my hands. Reach out your hand and put it into my side. Stop doubting and believe." Thomas said to him, "My Lord and my God!" (John 20:24-28)

2. **Reflection:** *Pray for Thomas to maintain his high standards for integrity. Ask God to help you be more open and appreciative of Thomas' "reality checks" in your life. Every few weeks, take the time for Thomas to give you a candid assessment of your organization and/or your leadership. Thank the Lord for Thomas.*

V. LIST THOMASES IN YOUR LIFE:

1. _____

2. _____

3. _____

4. _____

5. _____

VI. WHAT ACTION ARE YOU ARE YOU GOING TO TAKE
     THAT WILL SHOW YOUR UNCONDITIONAL LOVE
     AND FORGIVENESS OF THESE INDIVIDUALS?

     1. _____

     2. _____

     3. _____

     4. _____

     5. _____

THE FOOT WASHING PROJECT

DAY SIX: FRIDAY

I. FOCUS: Wash the feet of the other disciples.

II. PEOPLE TO IDENTIFY: Those who fit the
    description of "other disciples" for you (see
    Chapter 8).

III. PRACTICAL THING TO DO: Clarify the value and
     importance of at least one such person today,
     and tell them about it (note what you will say
     here):
     1. _____
     2. _____
     3. _____
     4. _____
     5. _____

IV. PRAYER APPROPRIATE FOR TODAY: Pray for each
    one by name, asking God to help them feel
    more a part of His work on earth, and of His
    work with you.

1. **Scripture:** *To the Jews who believed him, Jesus said, "If you hold to my teaching, you are really my disciples. Then you will know the truth, and the truth will set you free."* (John 8:31)

2. **Reflection:** *Pray for these people to hold to Jesus' teaching, and to integrity and faithfulness in their roles, as you encounter them in your life and organization. Pray that you can help clarify those roles in some way today. Pray for them by name if possible, that they might gain a greater understanding of the difference their faithful service can make in their current contexts.*

VI. List individuals you need to draw near and walk with like Jesus on the Emmaus Road (Luke 24):

1. _____

2. _____

3. _____

4. _____

5. _____

DAY SEVEN: SATURDAY

I. FOCUS: Wash the feet of Judas.

II. PERSON TO IDENTIFY: The person who functions as Judas in your life (see Chapter 9).

III. PRACTICAL THING TO DO: Look for an opportunity to be reconciled.

IV. PRAYER APPROPRIATE FOR TODAY: Pray that you will respond with grace toward your "Judas" and that you will trust this person in his/her daily role.

1. **Scripture:** *Six days before the Passover, Jesus arrived at Bethany, where Lazarus lived, whom Jesus had raised from the dead. Here a dinner was given in Jesus' honor. Martha served, while Lazarus was among those reclining at the table with him. Then Mary took about a pint of pure nard, an expensive perfume; she poured it on Jesus' feet and wiped his feet with her hair. And the house was filled with the fragrance of*

113

perfume. But one of the disciples, Judas Iscariot, who was later to betray him, objected, "Why wasn't this perfume sold and the money given to the poor? It was worth a year's wages!" He did not say this because he cared about the poor but because he was a thief; as keeper of the money bag, he used to help himself to what was in the money bag. "Leave her alone," Jesus replied. "It was intended that she should save this perfume for the day of my burial. You will always have the poor among you, but you will not always have me." (John 12:1-8)

2. **Reflection:** *Pray that the Judas in your life will develop a sincere heart for the needs of others. Ask God to reveal to you any way in which Judas might feel slighted somehow, and work to correct the issue. Pray for strength and commitment to wash this individual's feet until the end, and for grace to trust him with significant responsibilities. Pray, too, that there still might be a way to be reconciled.*

V. LIST JUDASES IN YOUR LIFE:

1. _____

2. _____

3. _____

4. _____

5. _____

VI. ASK THE LORD TO GIVE YOU HIS HEART SO THAT
     YOU CAN PUT YOUR HEART ABOVE YOUR HEAD BY
     SHOWING THESE INDIVIDUALS TRUE LOVE TILL THE
     END AND UNCONDITIONAL FORGIVENESS.

IS YOUR HEART SET ON SERVING?

Shortly after the War Between the States ended in the United States, a black man entered an Episcopalian church in Richmond, Virginia for the worship service. He was the only person of color in the building.

The congregation was still smarting from being a part of the Confederacy, the losing side of the conflict. Many people in the church were still prejudiced against black people. The feeling was only intensified for many of them as they approached the time for communion. When the black worshiper walked down the aisle to receive the elements, whispers were heard throughout the sanctuary. "We use a common cup! How disgraceful to share it with the likes of him!"

Almost immediately, one of the church's most respected leaders stood up and walked to the altar. He knelt to receive communion beside the black man, sharing the cup with him. Then he turned and addressed the congregation. "All men are brothers in Christ. Have we not all one Father?"

The man was the most famous general of the Confederacy, Robert E. Lee. The rest of the gathered

116

"*Blessed are the pure in heart,*
for they will see God."
Matthew 5:8

REFERENCES

[1] *The Online Bible Thayer's Greek Lexicon and Brown Driver & Briggs Hebrew Lexicon,* Copyright © 1993, Woodside Bible Fellowship, Ontario, Canada.

[2] William Barclay, *The Daily Study Bible: The Gospel of John,* Westminster Press, 1958).

[3] (International Standard Bible Encyclopedia, Electronic Database Copyright © 1996, 2003, 2006 by Biblesoft, Inc. All rights reserved.)